The Bluebird of
HAPPINESS

The Bluebird of Happiness

07 08 09 10 11 TWP 10 9 8 7 6 5 4 3

ISBN-13: 978-0-7407-6369-4
ISBN-10: 0-7407-6369-5

Library of Congress Control Number: 2006932267

www.andrewsmcmeel.com

The Bluebird of HAPPINESS

A Little Book of Cheer

Vicky Howard

Andrews McMeel
Publishing, LLC

Kansas City

Life is sweet, tender and complete,
when you find the bluebird of happiness.

—"Bluebird of Happiness,"
lyrics by Edward Heyman and Harry Parr Davies

What does it mean to be happy? In its broadest sense, happiness is a term for all that is good in life. Nothing guarantees us happiness, so we owe it to ourselves to live mindfully and to relish the special moments and experiences that bring us joy. Love and friendship are the foundations of happiness, but great pleasure can be found in the smallest things. When we pause in our busy day and observe the beauty found in nature, we lift our spirits and calm our fears. The heavenly scent of a rose and the beautiful song of the bluebird are reminders of the small miracles that can transform our daily lives.

The bluebird has long been considered a symbol of happiness and a messenger of joy and contentment. Birds and butterflies were beloved during the Victorian era, and the illustrations within are beautiful examples of the works of the finest artists of the period. Many of the accompanying poems were first printed in the early 1900s. A century later, our lives have changed dramatically but our observations on what encompasses a happy life have remained constant. It is my hope that this book, like the bluebird's song of happiness, will bring cheer and joy to your life.

*T*HE ART OF BEING HAPPY

LIES IN THE POWER

OF EXTRACTING HAPPINESS

FROM COMMON THINGS.

—Henry Ward Beecher

The best remedy
  for those who are afraid, lonely,
    or unhappy is to go outside . . .

amidst the simple beauty
of nature.

—Anne Frank

Those who contemplate

the beauty of the earth

find reserves of strength

that will endure

as long as life lasts.

—Rachel Louise Carson

Happiness . . .

not in another place

but this place,

not for another hour

but this hour.

—Walt Whitman

Today, whatever may annoy,

The word for me is joy, just simple joy:

The joy of bright blue skies;

The joy of rain; the glad surprise

Of twinkling stars that shine at night;

The joy of winged things upon their flight;

Whatever there be of sorrow

I'll put off until tomorrow!

—John Kendrick Bangs

*G*od bless the heart of sunshine
That smiles the clouds away,
And sets a star of fresh-born hope
In someone's sky each day.

God bless all words of kindness
That lifts the heart from gloom,
And in life's barren places
Plant flowers of love to bloom.

—A.H.G., *Book of Good Cheer*, 1913

*I*F WE MAKE IT OUR GOAL

TO LIVE A LIFE OF COMPASSION

AND UNCONDITIONAL LOVE,

THEN THE WORLD WILL INDEED

BECOME A GARDEN WHERE ALL

KINDS OF FLOWERS CAN

BLOOM AND GROW.

—Elisabeth Kübler-Ross

There is beauty in the sunlight,

And the soft blue heavens above;

Oh, the world is full of beauty

When the heart is full of love.

—*Kansas Second Reader, 1922*

Get into the habit of looking
for the silver lining of the cloud,
and when you have found it,
continue to look at it rather than
at the gray in the middle.

—A.A.W., *Book of Good Cheer*, 1922

It is not raining rain to me,
It's raining daffodils,
In every dimpled drop I see
Wildflowers on the hills

The shades of gray engulf the day
And overwhelm the town;
It is not raining rain to me,
It's raining roses down.

—Robert Loveman

*E*very year has its winter,
And every year has its rain—
But a day is always coming
When the birds fly north again.

It's the sweetest thing to remember
If courage is on the wane,
When the cold, dark days are over—
The birds will fly north again.

—Ella Higginson

Clouds may come, but clouds must go,
And they have a silver lining.
For beyond them all, you know,
Either sun or moon is shining.

—F.A.W., *Book of Good Cheer*, 1913

Whether the world

is blue or rosy

depends upon the kind

of spectacles we wear.

It's our glasses, not the world,

that need attention.

—Unknown

*I*F YOU COUNT THE SUNNY

AND THE CLOUDY DAYS OF

THE WHOLE YEAR, YOU WILL FIND

THAT THE SUNSHINE PREDOMINATES.

—Ovid

It's a beautiful world to see,
Or it's dismal in every zone;
The thing it must be
In your gloom or your glee
Depends on yourself alone.

—S. E. Kiser

There are two ways to live your life.

One is as though nothing is a miracle.

*The other is as though
everything is a miracle.*

—Albert Einstein

When I first

open my eyes upon

the morning meadows

and look out upon

the beautiful world,

I thank God I am alive.

—Ralph Waldo Emerson

T his is the best day
the world has ever seen.
Tomorrow will be better.

—R. A. Campbell, *Just Being Happy*, 1913

Write it on your heart

that every day is the

best day of the year.

—Ralph Waldo Emerson

If you have a song to sing,
Sing it now.
Let the tones of gladness ring
Clear as song of bird in spring.
Let every day some music bring;
Sing it now.

If you have a smile to show,
Show it now.
Make hearts happy, roses grow,
Let the friends around you know
The love you have before they go;
Show it now.

—Unknown, *Book of Good Cheer*, 1913

It's loving and giving

that make life worth living.

—Proverb

*L*ittle deeds of kindness,

Little words of love,

Help to make earth happy

Like the heavens above.

—Julia Fletcher Carney,
ABC Lesson Book, 1860

Celebrate golden days,
fruitful of golden deeds,
With joy and love triumphing.

—John Milton

Half the world is on the wrong scent in the pursuit of happiness. They think it consists in having and getting, and in being served by others. It consists in giving and in serving others.

—Henry Drummond,
Just Being Happy, 1913

We must be purposely
kind and generous or we miss
the best part of life's existence.
The heart that goes out of itself
gets large and full of joy.
We do ourselves the most good
by doing something for others.

—Horace Mann

Happiness is the only good.
The place to be happy is here.
The time to be happy is now.

The way to be happy is to
help make others so.

—Robert G. Ingersoll

*Y*OU CANNOT ALWAYS *have* HAPPINESS,

BUT YOU CAN ALWAYS *give* HAPPINESS.

—Proverb

No one has the right

to consume happiness

without producing it.

—Helen Keller

Not what we have, but what we use;

Not what we see, but what we choose—

These are the things that mar or bless

The sum of human happiness.

—Unknown, *Just Being Happy*, 1913

WE MAKE A LIVING BY

WHAT WE GET,

BUT WE MAKE A LIFE

BY WHAT WE GIVE.

—Sir Winston Churchill

If you want to understand
the meaning of happiness,

you must see it as a reward

and not as a goal.

—Antoine de Saint-Exupéry

God gives every bird

his worm, but he does not

throw it into the nest.

—Swedish Proverb

A happy life is one
which is in accordance with
its own nature.

—Lucius Annaeus Seneca

We live in an ascending scale when we live happily, one thing leading to another in an endless series.

—Robert Louis Stevenson

$\mathcal{H}$appiness lies in the joy of achievement and the thrill of creative effort.

—Franklin Roosevelt

$\mathcal{N}$o pessimist ever discovered

the secrets of the stars,

or sailed to an uncharted land,

or opened a new heaven

to the horizon of the spirit.

—Helen Keller

W*here your pleasure is,*

there is your treasure;

where your treasure is,

there your heart;

where your heart,

there your happiness.

—Saint Augustine

The best and most beautiful things in the world cannot be seen or even touched. They must be felt with the heart.

—Helen Keller

$\mathcal{H}$appiness in this world,

when it comes, comes incidentally.

Follow some other object,

and very possibly we may find

that we have caught

happiness without dreaming of it.

—Nathaniel Hawthorne

The bird of happiness

lights only upon the hand

that does not grasp.

—John Berry

Happiness is a butterfly
which, when pursued, is always
beyond our grasp, but which,
if you sit down quietly,
may alight upon you.

—Nathaniel Hawthorne